Corporate Physics

Corporate Physics

Accelerating Change . . . to Achieve
a Result . . . that Satisfies a Need

John Calvello

VANTAGE PRESS
New York

Published by Vantage Press, Inc.
419 Park Ave. South, New York, NY 10016

Manufactured in the United States of America
ISBN: 978-0-533-15931-4

Library of Congress Catalog Card No.: 2007908409

0 9 8 7 6 5 4 3 2 1

To my wife, Mary Anne,
and to my daughters, Kristina and Angela

Contents

Introduction

I wrote *Corporate Physics* to give business Leaders a framework and means of **accelerating Change, to achieve a result, that satisfies a need.**

The book can be utilized by Leaders at all levels within the business environment who need to meet the never-ending challenges that come with competing in our global economy. Whether you're a Chairman of the Board, a CEO, a first-line supervisor, or anyone in between, my goal is to help you become a more effective Leader. And make no mistake about it, <u>Leadership</u> is the key ingredient to competing successfully.

Whether you're a Leader who needs to demonstrate continuous quarterly EBITDA (Earnings Before Interest, Taxes, Depreciation and Armortization) <u>growth</u> to "The Street," or a Leader who needs to <u>improve</u> the on-time quality throughput of your department, the act of <u>growing</u> or <u>improving</u> implies Change. As competition evolves and becomes more formidable, your proven ability to accelerate Change will help your company become more competitive and help **you** become a more competitive and marketable Leader.

So good luck and may the Force be with you!

Corporate Physics

Prologue

Physics is not a subject that most people leap to pursue. Most people who have taken at least one Physics course find it to be too technical, intimidating or even just plain torture. I can personally attest to the latter. You see, many years ago, as an aspiring Industrial Engineer at Purdue University, Physics was *the* "flunk-out" course for freshmen would-be engineers of all types. It was the kind of course where the average score on any given exam was 26 out of 100 points, and an "A" was any score above a 42. I hated Physics!

Yes, hate is a strong word. But at that time, that's how felt about Physics and all of its "spin-off" related courses, like Statics, Dynamics, Strength of Materials, Thermo Dynamics, Heat Transfer, Fluid Mechanics . . . well, you get the picture. All of those torture chamber courses were highly technical requirements toward earning an engineering degree at Purdue. So even though I perceived these high-tech courses to be irrelevant in helping me to solve business problems, which is where my interest lay, they were required to earn any type of engineering degree from Purdue.

Industrial Engineering is fun! It is also commonly misunderstood by the general public, industry, and even by business consultants. You know; "those are the time study experts." This book will not try to educate you on the value of Industrial Engineering, so let's just suffice to say that Industrial Engineering incorporates a vast range of disciplines and techniques applied to businesses, focused on *accelerating Change, to achieve a result, that satisfies a need.* So I endured Physics and all the rest of those "irrelevant" courses to earn my Bachelor of Science degree in Industrial Engineering.

A year after graduation, I had the opportunity to vacation in London with a close friend. We enjoyed the sites of London during the day and the theatre at night. One day, while touring Westminster Abbey, I stumbled onto the grave of Sir Isaac Newton. For those of you who don't know, or may not recall, Isaac Newton was the scientist from the seventeenth century who developed the basic principles of Physics. Newtonian Physics has been universally taught for centuries, and has withstood the rigorous proofs of time to evolve into scientific laws. Although Albert Einstein's theories of relativity have greatly expanded upon Newton's Laws, Newtonian Physics is still taught in institutions of higher learning around the world. I was taught Newtonian Physics!

So there I stood staring down at Sir Isaac Newton's grave, with my college experience still very fresh in mind. I flashed back to the strain from the long hours of study; the anxiety of having to face the upcoming exams; the stress of realizing I didn't have a clue on how to approach three of the four problems on any exam; and the anger of thinking that I would never use any of that "knowledge" again. When I snapped back out of that horrifying flashback, I thought to myself, "So you're the son-of-a-bitch that put me through that living hell." I felt satisfied, having given Sir Isaac a piece of my mind "face-to-face" so to speak. But I felt even more satisfied thinking that the role of physics in my life was as dead and buried as Sir Isaac Newton. Boy, was I wrong!

Many years had passed since my "meeting" with Sir Isaac Newton. After spending several years in a dynamic "fast-track" career path in industry, I joined a top-flight implementation management consulting firm. I have had what many people would consider to be a very successful and rewarding career in consulting. I have been lucky enough to be part of cutting-edge approaches that have helped my clients to become more competitive and profitable. My early successes were achieved without ever thinking about Physics.

However, in one of my programs for the flagship division of a Fortune 500, U.S.-based company, progress was very slow in coming. Our project team was having great trouble in affecting Change within this organization. The behaviors of the people we were working with were extremely closed. Resistance to Change was extraordinarily high. The tension between the client's organization and our project team was so severe that the success of the program and even its very existence were in jeopardy. I spent many sleepless nights tossing and turning, wondering how to overcome this situation and get this program back on track.

Prior to going to work one morning, my mind was once again totally consumed with the dilemma I was facing. I was pondering why we could not get this organization to Change. The organization was clearly not moving in the direction it needed to go to become more competitive and profitable. In fact, it was not moving at all. It was seemingly at rest and we hadn't applied the right types or amount of Force to get it to move or, in other words, to Change. And then one of the fundamental laws of Physics occurred to me, "A body in motion tends to stay in motion and a body at rest tends to stay at rest." Newton! Could Physics help me to find the answer?

When I returned home that weekend, I borrowed an old Physics textbook from a friend who actually kept hers (I had gleefully sold mine back to one of the campus book stores years ago), and re-examined many of the principles and formulas in a different light. It was truly amazing to me to discover how many of these principles and formulas actually applied to implementing Changes within corporate organizations. For example, there are terms, concepts and formulas in Newtonian Physics dealing with displacement (the direction and magnitude of Change), velocity, inertia, acceleration, mass, Force, friction, work, energy, power, momentum, impulse, torque, elasticity, stress, strain, strength, yield point and pressure; all descriptors of organizational characteristics while transforming during the Change process. But don't worry, I'm not going to take you through the same technical tortures I experienced in college.

Using the simplest and most fundamental of these laws from Newtonian Physics helped me to crystallize my thinking at that time and helped guide me to turn that program around. The result was a more competitive and profitable client. Since that engagement, not one client intervention has gone by in my career without my mentally applying Newton's most fundamental law, $F = ma$, Force equals mass times acceleration. It has provided me with a framework for *accelerating Change, to achieve a result, that satisfies a need,* which has greatly benefited my clients' companies over the years.

acceleration

1

Change

What is Change?

If our friend Sir Isaac were still alive, he would instruct us that Change is to business as *displacement* is to Physics. If you don't remember, or never took Physics, displacement is the difference between two points, let's say, Point A and Point B. Displacement is typically depicted by an arrow between the two points, called a vector, containing two properties, namely, *direction* and *magnitude*. So displacement is the difference in direction and magnitude, or *Change,* required to go from Point A to Point B.

Simply put, Change is the difference between two points in terms of direction and magnitude:

Change = (Point B) – (Point A)

In figure 1.1 on the next page, six examples of Change are shown. The first three cases show examples of physical Changes which you may expect would be reviewed in a Physics class. The next three cases show examples of Changes that top executives, middle managers, first line supervisors and work forces strive to achieve in the business world.

But why Change?

Figure 1.1: Examples of Change

Point A	Point B	Change	
		Direction	Magnitude
	- Physical Examples -		
Chicago	New York	East	700 miles
Freezing	Boiling	Warmer	100° Celsius
200 lbs.	175 lbs.	Lighter	25 lbs.
	- Business Examples -		
$100 cost per unit	$50 cost per unit	Lower	$50 per unit
65% on-time deliveries	95% on-time deliveries	Higher	30%
2% EBITDA	10% EBITDA	Higher	8%

Businesses have many reasons for Changing. If your business can not meet either market place demands or competition relative to: 1) the types of products or services offered, 2) the quality and reliability of those products or services, 3) productivity and cost, 4) price, or 5) timeliness and completeness of delivery, then the survival of your business is in jeopardy. For many companies, their ultimate survival is dependent upon their ability to Change from Point A, the way they do business today, to Point B, a new way of doing business to better meet market place demands and the threats of increased competition.

For example, let's say your company produces the right products, of the highest quality and reliability, at a low cost and sells them at competitive prices. However, you do not enjoy the major share of the market because your deliveries are not as timely as the competition's. Your customers are telling you that unless you reduce your delivery cycle from three weeks to one week, they will give your share of their business to your competition.

What would you do? That's right; find a way to reduce your delivery cycle from three weeks to one week. This Change is necessary to survive in the marketplace.

For other companies, growth is the motivation to Change. Most investors and financial analysts judge a business's success based upon its ability to continually grow the company's earnings, often times on a quarter-to-quarter basis. This earnings growth objective often becomes a personal job survival issue for the company's top executives who cannot implement the Changes necessary to achieve the growth objectives within the expected time.

More and more investment banking and private equity firms are buying companies with the intention of executing an equity event, like an initial public offering of stock (IPO) or by simply reselling ("flipping") them in three to five years to create an attractive return on their original investment. Their target companies are those with high potential to grow earnings before interest, taxes, depreciation and amortization (EBITDA) or earnings per share (EPS) by applying significant Changes in the target company's operating and financial structure. And conversely, the best means for a business to avoid becoming the target of unwanted new ownership is to continually Change to grow earnings at the maximum rate possible.

In addition to survival and growth, there are many other reasons why businesses are motivated to Change. Some companies may want to Change to enhance their status, image or power. Others may want to Change to better serve their community or protect the environment. And I am sure there are many other reasons that motivate businesses to Change. However, the two primary motivators for businesses to Change that I have encoun-

Figure 1.2: Hierarchy of Business Needs

tered over the years have been survival and growth. Reminiscent of Maslow, Figure 1.2 shows the hierarchy of businesses' needs for Change.

Over time, market trends shift, customers become more demanding and competition becomes more formidable. In this dynamic business environment, the Change that surrounds companies is never-ending. So companies must Change accordingly in order to compete. Otherwise they will not grow and may not even survive.

In my experience, the ability to Change is the most valuable competitive weapon that a company can possess.

2
Rate of Change

What is the Rate of Change?

In Physics, Newton would have told us that *velocity* is an example of the rate of Change. Velocity (v) is equivalent to the amount of Displacement (D) experienced over a specific period of time (t), or, $v = D/t$. Chapter 1 taught us that, in business, Change is the substitute for Displacement. The Rate of Change (r) is equivalent to the experienced Change (C) over a specific period of time (t), or, $r = C/t$.

Continuing on with the examples shown in Figure 1.1, and given hypothetical time periods, Figure 2.1 shows the calculated Rate of Change for each example.

Figure 2.1: Examples of Rate of Change

Change		Time Period	Rate of Change
Direction	Magnitude		
- Physical Examples -			
East	700 miles	14 hours	50 mph east
Warmer	100° Celsius	10 hours	10° C per hour warmer
Lighter	25 lbs.	5 weeks	5 lbs. per week lighter
- Business Examples -			
Lower	$50 per unit	10 years	$5 per year lower unit cost
Higher	30%	6 years	5% per year higher on-time deliveries
Higher	8%	4 years	2% per year higher EBITDA

In Figure 2.1 on the previous page, the six examples of Rate of Change are calculated by simply dividing the Change by the time period involved. Notice that Rates of Change contain components of direction, magnitude and time. This will always be the case, with no exceptions.

Why is the Rate of Change important?

In Chapter 1, we discussed the reasons why Change is important for a company to survive and grow. But, if enacted over too long a period of time, the Change will fall short of what is needed to compete. Your customers won't wait forever!

Time is powerful. We can't touch it, taste it, smell it, hear it or see it. Yet it is there, continually marching on. We can't speed it up or slow it down. When competing, it can be your ally if you are ahead, or it can be your enemy if you are behind.

In order to be a viable and growing concern, a company must harness time by continually being capable of achieving a higher Rate of Change than its competitors.

3

Acceleration

What is acceleration?

Simply put, acceleration is an increase in the Rate of Change.

Two of Newton's laws, in layman's terms, are: 1) a body in motion tends to stay in motion and 2) a body at rest tends to stay at rest. He was referring to the concept of *inertia* as it pertains to physical masses or objects.

Unless some extraordinary influence or Force is applied to an object that is moving at a certain speed, its velocity (Rate of Change) will continue at that speed. Similarly, unless some extraordinary influence or Force is applied to an object that is not moving, its velocity (Rate of Change) will continue to be zero.

In our previous three physical examples, each of the three rates of Change could be increased by applying an extraordinary influence or Force. One could travel from Chicago to New York in half the time, seven hours, by pressing the *"accelerator"* down to make the car's velocity (Rate of Change) 100 mph as opposed to 50 mph (watch out for Smokeys!). Similarly, one could turn up the burner to achieve the 100°C temperature increase faster. And one could even undergo liposuction to remove the twenty-five pounds faster than dieting and exercising alone.

Well, guess what? The same laws apply in business. Companies have inertia too. In the three previous business examples, the respective rates of Change of $5 per year lower unit cost, 5 percent per year higher on-time deliveries and 2 percent per year higher EBITDA may not be large enough to remain competitive or keep new owners away.

A company will not experience an increased growth rate without applying some extraordinary influence or Force to accelerate the Rate of Change. This could come in the form of a new product introduction, shifting product sourcing to low-cost global regions, implementing a successful productivity improvement initiative, etc. In fact, if no extraordinary influence or Force is applied, a company's growth rate is in jeopardy of degrading as competitors apply their own actions to accelerate Changes in their companies.

To increase the Rate of Change in a company, let's refer back to our friend Sir Isaac Newton. One of his most famous formulas in the field of Physics is **F=ma,** or Force equals mass times acceleration. By flipping the formula around, we can see that **a=F/m,** or:

acceleration = Force ÷ mass

So acceleration in the Rate of Change will increase as Force increases or as mass decreases. However, acceleration will decrease as Force decreases or mass increases.

Another way of thinking about this is, the larger the mass, then the larger the Force needs to be to overcome that mass in order to increase the Rate of Change.

In the six examples we have studied so far, be they physical examples or business examples, Force was applied to increase the Rate of Change in situations where the current *inertia* was going in the intended direction. But what if the *inertia* was zero, or even worse, going in the opposite direction? Then it takes significantly more Force to turn the situation around and accelerate Change in the right direction.

Let's take the Chicago to New York example. If instead of heading toward New York, let's say you were heading toward Denver. You would have to apply the brakes, then turn the car around and, depending on how far west you had already traveled, press the "*accelerator*" to well over 100 mph to arrive in New York in seven hours.

Again, the same is true in business. For example, if a company is losing money, it will require much more Force to turn the company around and achieve the earnings needed to survive and grow, as compared to a company that is already profitable.

Effective business Leaders exert the right kinds and amounts of Force to overcome the mass within their organizations to accelerate the Rate of Change, or more simply put, to accelerate Change. The true role of the business Leader is to apply the necessary Force for *accelerating Change, to achieve a result, that satisfies a need.*

So what is this Force we are talking about?

Before we get to that, let's examine what we mean by mass, as it pertains to business.

mass

4

People

The mass of a company is the summation of its critical components at any point in time. These critical components include people, structure, processes, systems and assets. Of these critical components of organizational mass, the most important is people. This is because people create or adjust the remaining critical components of a company.

When it comes to organizational *inertia,* the more people that are in a company, the more Force is required to accelerate Change. For example, a start-up company with ten employees is much more nimble and flexible than a huge and mature corporation of 100,000 employees. Remember, **acceleration = Force ÷ mass.**

To the extent that people are a critical component of a company's mass, a reduction in the sheer number of employees can go a long way to accelerate Change. The impact on earnings is immediate and "The Street" usually looks favorably upon such actions, typically causing share price to rise. This may sound cold and harsh, but remember, in this competitive global economy, it may be worth sacrificing some jobs to secure the majority of remaining jobs, improve earnings and provide a more attractive return to the company's investors. And once a company is financially healthy and competitive, its likely growth often causes more people to be hired than the number originally released.

People are often comfortable and secure with the position they're in, the work that they do, the status they have attained over the years, etc. It is oftentimes human nature to feel threatened by, and therefore resist, Change. Naturally, everyone is different and some people are more inflexible and resistant to Change than others.

I have worked with some companies where the union work rules were so inflexible and union leadership was so resistant to Change that their very resistance was the key contributor to losing many of their members' jobs to foreign workers. Happily, as time has progressed, I have found unions to be much more flexible and seeking to partner with company management to accelerate Change to remain competitive and viable.

People generally come to work to do a good job every day. They also like and need to be recognized for doing so. If they know what is expected of them, and receive recognition for doing it, they will typically meet or exceed expectations. I have found that this behavior also applies to a person's ability and willingness to Change.

The table in Figure 4.1 opposite is a tool that has been around for a long time that can be used to categorize people in terms of their ability and willingness to Change. If you believe, like I do, that a company's survival and growth depend upon its ability to accelerate Change, then the people component of a company's mass needs to be identified in terms of their ability and willingness to Change. People in the upper left-hand quadrant of Figure 4.1 are potential Leaders who can champion Change. They can become part of a company's Force.

People in the lower left-hand quadrant will require training to Change. People in the upper right-hand quad-

Figure 4.1: Ability and Willingness to Change

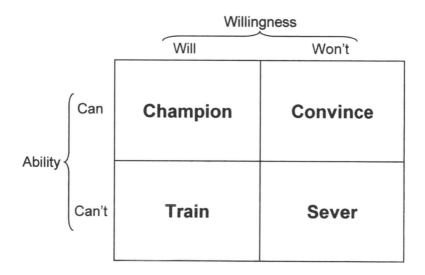

rant must be convinced to Change, and once there, my experience is that these people can become the biggest advocates for Change. People in the lower right-hand quadrant often need to be severed, as they can cause *friction* (another of Newton's terms) and become an impediment to Change. These people usually represent less than 5 percent of the population.

Another important phenomenon as it pertains to people and their willingness to Change, is the concept of ownership. It is human nature to want to make something succeed when they feel it is theirs. Ownership is a powerful motivator. This phenomenon also holds true for accelerating Change.

Figure 4.2 on the next page shows the linkage between ownership and Change:

Figure 4.2: The Ownership to Change Linkage

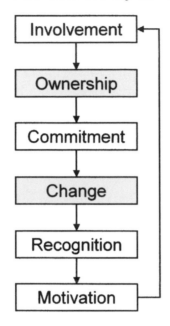

In the preceding illustration, involvement is a mandatory precursor for a person to feel ownership. People who are listened to and have a hand in shaping the Change have a higher probability of feeling ownership for the Change. As in other aspects of life, like home ownership, authorship and advancing ideas, ownership breeds pride and commitment. The higher the level of commitment, the higher the probability of successfully accelerating Change. And once recognized for achieving the Change, people become motivated to become even more involved.

The degree to which the above behavioral chain either exists or doesn't exist is a pivotal characteristic of the people component of a company's mass.

5

Structure

Organization structure is a second critical component of a company's mass and is very closely related to the people component. After all, organization structure is how people are grouped together to run the company. When you think about organization structure, think about the traditional box and wire diagrams that depict them. But one must also consider the relative roles, responsibilities, accountabilities and authority associated with each position in the structure.

The organization structure in small companies is typically less formal and more flexible than in large companies. In small companies, everyone tends to pitch in and do whatever it takes to get the job done. This can be a tremendous advantage for small companies. However, that same feature, if applied to large companies or corporations, can cause anarchy, chaos and become a tremendous disadvantage.

Large companies and corporations tend to organize in specialized groupings of people called functions, departments, project teams, business units, divisions and shared services, to name just a few. Each specialized grouping of people tends to focus on either a specific customer segment, a geographical market, a product line or service offering, or a core competency. Each specialized grouping is to work together for the betterment of the company as a whole.

The organization structures in large companies and corporations evolve over time and, quite often, take their shape as a result of some strong personalities. For example, the ex-president of an acquired business may have tremendous power to influence the resulting structure due to his or her strong relationships with the acquired company's customer base. Or a strong aerospace program manager may exert his or her power to cherry-pick the company's best engineering talent to staff their program over a multiple-year timeframe.

These are just two examples of literally hundreds of potential scenarios where strong individuals can heavily influence organization structure. This is not unnatural, as it is people who create structure. But there will always be the chance that individuals will create structures that promote their own recognition and betterment to the potential detriment of the company as a whole. The need to perpetuate their structures by these strong personalities, often called "protecting one's turf," can become a huge impediment to Change.

As part of my education as an Industrial Engineer, I was taught the old axiom that "form follows function." This axiom holds true almost universally, but not necessarily when it comes to accelerating Change in relation to organization structure. Instinctively, one would expect that newly designed business processes (to be discussed in the next chapter) should occur first. Then the organization structure should be designed to support the new processes, hence, "form follows function."

This is not always the case. I have experienced numerous occasions where the current organization structure is such an impediment to accelerating Change in business processes, that restructuring needed to occur first in order to facilitate the implementation of the new processes. Sometimes you have to break a few eggs to make an omelet!

The opposite of specialized groupings within an organization structure that have too much power are those that don't have enough power. Many times I have seen specialized groupings be held accountable to accelerate Change without the commensurate authority to impact the Change. This is particularly true of staff positions in highly matrixed organizations where, at best, only influence can be exerted over line or P&L groupings. Unless anointed with special authority by ultimate decision-makers, these positions of mere influence are most likely doomed to failure when it comes to accelerating Change.

Another important aspect of a company's mass, as it pertains to organization structure, is the structure's size and shape in terms of the number of organizational levels, spans-of-control and complexity. Similar to our discussion of the sheer number of people in the previous chapter, the same argument applies to the size of an organization structure. Remembering our fundamental formula of **acceleration = Force ÷ mass**, the larger and more complex a company's structure is, the more difficult it will be accelerate Change.

The example in Figure 5.1 (page 26) shows a three-to-one (3:1) span-of-control.

The rule of thumb, as it pertains to span-of-control, is that a ratio of at least 7:1 direct reports to each Leader within an organization structure is desirable. This rule of thumb needs to be tempered, however, by geography and by the variety and complexity of the jobs being managed.

If a Leader is managing people who perform the same

25

repetitive tasks in a confined space, then the span-of-control can be significantly higher than 7:1. On the other hand, if a Leader is managing a variety of complex jobs across a large geographic region, then perhaps a 7:1 span-of-control is too large. The span-of-control needs to be judged on a case-by-case basis, based upon the capacity of the Leader to provide the proper amounts of supervision to his or her direct reports.

The histogram in Figure 5.2 opposite shows the actual span-of-control profile, at that time, for a division of a major electronics corporation.

Figure 5.1: Sample Organization Structure

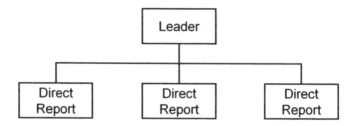

The histogram shows that sixteen Leaders within the organization structure managed only one person. Another twenty-one Leaders managed only two people. Twenty-five Leaders managed only three people, etc. As can be seen, two thirds (66 percent) of the Leaders within that division had a span-of-control of 5:1 or less.

In this example, the spans-of-control are skewed too far to the left, indicating that the organization structure contains too many people. Simply put, this organization structure is top-heavy. And remembering our fundamental formula of **acceleration = Force ÷ mass**, this com-

Figure 5.2: Span-of-Control Profile

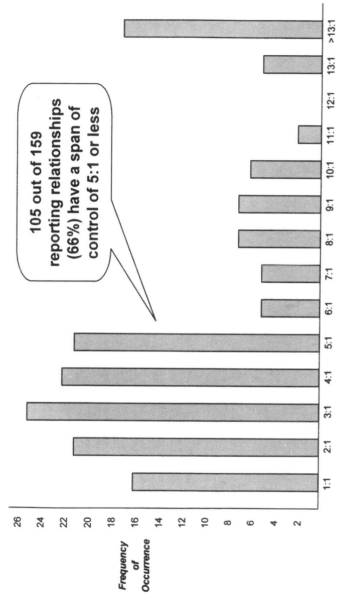

105 out of 159 reporting relationships (66%) have a span of control of 5:1 or less

pany's organization structure is an impediment to accelerating Change.

Small spans-of-control also impact the number of levels within an organization structure. The smaller the spans-of-control, the deeper a company will be in terms of the organizational levels between the CEO or President, and the front-line worker. Conversely, the larger the spans-of-control, the flatter the organization structure will be. Flatter organizations facilitate shorter lines of communications from top to bottom and are more mobile when it comes to accelerating Change.

6

Processes

Much has been written about business processes, from Reengineering to Lean Manufacturing, Lean Office and Lean Enterprise. Information abounds on value-added steps versus non-value added steps and value-stream mapping. So I will not attempt to "reinvent the wheel" regarding business processes in this chapter. For our purposes, let's just define a business process as the steps required to produce a deliverable to either an external or internal "customer" of the process.

Having said that, business processes are one of the critical components that comprise a company's mass.

Like the other components of a company's mass, processes tend to have their own *inertia*. It's difficult for me to recount the number of times my client's response to the question "Why do you do it like that?" is "Because we've always done it that way." That response screams for the need for process redesign to accelerate Change.

Occasionally, processes and the cost to perform them exist that add no value at all. At one of my clients, a woman spent a large percentage of her time producing a report that she then deposited in her personal file. When I asked her why she did that, she said the report was for a previous boss who wanted it, but that he had been gone for two years! Even though the current boss didn't ask for the report, the woman kept on producing it because, "I've always done it."

At a chemical manufacturer, an entire process existed to wash bottles that were filled with a heavy liquid for their customers. The heavy liquid had to be very sterile, requiring an extremely low particulate count. The bottle-washing process was utilized, even though the bottles that were delivered to them were purported to being sterilized by their supplier. After the company's manufacturing engineers performed extensive testing, the unwashed bottles from the supplier were found to be cleaner, with a lower particulate count, than the washed bottles!

The bottle-washing process and its associated costs were swiftly eliminated by the chemical manufacturer. It should be noted that the impetus that launched this process improvement occurred after one of the workers who actually performed the job was taught to ask the question "Why?" In this case he asked, "Why do we wash the bottles when they supposedly come to us from our supplier already sterilized?"

The bottle-washer example points to an important characteristic of a company's mass that involves the intersection of processes and people. This intersection deals with the extent to which processes are routinely questioned as to why they are done that way or even at all, and the involvement of the people who actually do the work in that questioning. To the extent that this does not routinely occur, this intersection void adds to the company's mass. To the extent that it does routinely occur, this intersection can be transformed into a Force to accelerate Change.

Large companies and corporations have literally hundreds of processes. Although all of them are important, assuming they add value, the most important processes are those that directly interface with external customers and clients. After all, it's customers and clients who will ultimately determine a company's survival, growth and need to accelerate Change.

And of the processes that directly interface with external customers and clients, the processes that develop and introduce the products and services that are consumed in the competitive marketplace are the most important. Too often, I have seen companies that are not developing and introducing the products or services that the marketplace wants and needs. These companies often suffer from the long-term *inertia* of being either product-driven or engineering-driven.

These types of companies tend to engineer new products and services whether the marketplace needs them or not. Now don't get me wrong; I'm not knocking engineers. Remember, I am an engineer by education. And good engineers are arguably the most valuable and precious resource in the development process—just ask the Chinese, Japanese and Koreans, who mint as many new engineers as fast as they can, many in U.S. schools.

Companies who have a track record of success (survive and grow), employ processes that focus their precious technical resources on developing and introducing products and services that are market-needs-driven. They employ these processes in a timely fashion to beat their competition and win market share. So speed to market, the Rate of Change to introduce new products and services, is perhaps the highest priority process within a company's mass.

31

7

Systems

There are two types of systems when considering a company's mass, namely, information systems and managing systems.

Information systems are certainly required to support the day-to-day running of all key business functions, such as marketing, sales, operations, finance, etc. Like business processes, legacy information systems have their own *inertia* and tend to evolve over time. These legacy information systems are typically cumbersome and expensive to run and maintain.

Companies have spent multiples of 10's and 100's of millions of dollars in implementing new systems to replace their legacy information systems. This is true, particularly in the case of enterprise resource planning (ERP) systems. Unfortunately, too many of these implementations either have not demonstrated any return on investment, or have caused major disruptions to the company's business. Some have even been total failures, resulting in their abandonment and the loss of many executives' jobs who promoted them.

My IT friends may not like my saying this, but information systems are a part of a company's mass and are not a driving Force for accelerating Change!

Managing systems are the means by which the performance of people, organization structures, processes and assets get measured and Changed. So, by definition, an effective managing system can be a driving Force for accelerating Change. On the other hand, an incomplete or ineffective managing system becomes another component of a company's mass and an inhibitor of Change.

The major elements of a managing system are goals, performance measurement, barrier identification, barrier removal, and reward and recognition. Goals typically have components of productivity, quality and customer service. Performance measurement is the means to track attainment of the goals, that may or may not be enabled through information systems. Barrier identification involves surfacing issues that are barriers to achieving the goals. Barrier removal is self-evident, as it speaks to the elimination of barriers. Reward and recognition is the means to motivate people to achieve and raise the goals.

The graphic in Figure 7.1 displays a "Closed-Loop Managing System":

Figure 7.1: Closed-Loop Managing System

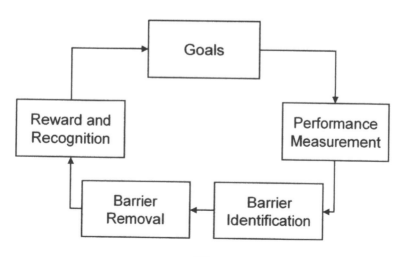

To the extent that the goals are "stretch goals" that aren't currently being achieved, then these goals incorporate the desired Change in both magnitude and direction. Therefore, an effective managing system is a driving Force for accelerating Change. And as stated earlier, an incomplete or ineffective managing system is just another component of a company's mass that inhibits Change.

8

Assets

So why are assets part of a company's mass? Aren't assets a good thing? Well, the answer is a resounding yes . . . and no!

When looking at a company's balance sheet, it will be divided into two sections, namely, an assets section, and a liabilities and equity section. The fundamental accounting formula for a balance sheet is: assets = liabilities + equity. This <u>balance</u> will always occur because, by definition, equity is the residual of claims on the assets of a business by its owners, left over, after the business has settled all claims held by outsiders, called liabilities.

Taking a closer look at the assets on a company's balance sheet, assets are broken down into two categories, namely, current assets and non-current assets. Current assets include Cash and other assets that can be directly exchanged for Cash, like accounts receivable and inventories. Non-current assets are those that can be used to generate Cash inflows indirectly, such as properties, plants and equipment, all of which are accounted for net of depreciation.

The main characteristic of assets is that a business can exchange them for Cash or use them to generate Cash inflows. Cash is good! "Cash is king." Making money is the reason that businesses exist. And Cash is absolutely a desirable asset that can be used as part of a company's Force to accelerate Change (more on this in Chapter 15).

But what about a company's assets other than Cash? Are they a positive Force to accelerate Change? Or are they part of a company's mass that inhibits Change? This is where it becomes a little murky.

To clear up the murkiness, let's start by examining one of the two major current assets, other than Cash, that being accounts receivable. Accounts receivable are a good thing. They are solid indicators that customers and clients are buying a company's goods and services. And accounts receivable can be directly exchanged for Cash, once collected. The "once collected" part of the previous sentence is where the rub comes in. In order to convert a receivable to Cash, a company has to be able to collect payment from their customers and clients.

Oftentimes, a company's customers and clients may be slow in paying their bills, or, due to their financial position, may not pay at all. Many companies expend much expense for employees and communications to recover collectables due to them. Some companies may even outsource their collections to a third party for a hefty commission, or even sell their receivables to a third party at a tremendous discount. Still other accounts receivable are never collected or outsourced, and are simply written off as bad debt.

These problematic receivables create expense, and therefore, mass within a company, and deteriorate the ability to generate Cash. Companies with effective credit screening business processes can minimize their risk of experiencing these problematic receivables. Also, the efficiency and effectiveness of a company's collection processes will have a direct impact on how much mass exists when it comes to managing this asset.

The second of the two major current assets, other than Cash, is inventory, which is comprised of raw materials, work-in-process and finished goods. Inventory is really tricky in a manufacturing company or retailer because they need to have the right finished goods available in the right quantities, at the right place, at the right time, in order to satisfy marketplace demand, generate Cash and avoid losing business to the competition. And for a manufacturing company, you can extend that same logic through the supply chain to work-in-process and raw materials in order to replenish finished goods.

Where it becomes tricky is to have the ability to satisfy demand without having too much inventory. Too much inventory adds to the mass of a company by consuming Cash that could otherwise be used for other investments. Too much inventory also leads to excessive expenses for handling and storage. It also adds to the potential for obsolete inventory that can not be exchanged for Cash, or if so, at a tremendous discount.

Like problematic receivables, excess inventory is symptomatic of ineffective and inefficient business processes. The inverse is also true, that is, in order to meet marketplace demand, excessive inventory is required to compensate for inefficient and ineffective business processes. In this case, the main culprits are the forecasting process, production planning and control, and distribution and logistics.

If a company could produce and deliver products within a timeframe that meets the needs of the customer expressed when they place their order, then finished goods inventory would not be necessary at all. These companies do exist! Lean manufacturing and "pull" processes can be employed to drive toward a zero finished goods environment. These Lean and "pull" processes are much simpler and less expensive to administer than "push" processes that are based on forecasting, and they also create much less excessive inventory mass.

Unlike the mass associated with the current assets of accounts receivable and inventories that are the result of inefficient and ineffective business processes, the mass associated with the non-current assets of properties, plants and equipment is more the result of inefficient and ineffective structure. Like many other components of a company's mass, oftentimes these non-current physical assets evolve over time and have their own *inertia*. However, at other times they are caused by the direct and intentional influence of people.

In Chapter 5, we talked about how organization structures evolve over time and how sometimes strong personalities can exert their will over the structure of the company. Oftentimes this phenomenon is exacerbated through acquisitions. Sometimes a strong personality will fight to maintain or expand the number of people that work for them in order to cement or build their power base.

The same phenomenon is true for non-current physical assets of a company. Some strong personalities will fight to maintain or expand the number of plants and equipment, warehouses, sales offices, regional offices, etc., under their control in order to cement or build their power base. The more matrixed the organization, with P&L leaders, functional leaders and geographic leaders, the higher the possibility that this can occur. And like structure, this phenomenon is exacerbated through acquisitions.

The right amount of non-current physical assets of a company is the amount necessary to meet the market rate of demand and grow the business. No more! To the extent that a company's physical footprint and capacity is more than is needed, that consumes Cash that could have been directed toward the true needs of the business and is definitely a large component of mass.

The one exception where some believe a non-current asset is part of a company's Force, rather than its mass, is equipment that is so technologically advanced that it differentiates the company's productivity, cost, quality and/or service from the competition. But technology can be copied, even when patents exist, particularly by non-U.S.-based companies. So it is the effective ongoing pursuit and implementation of differentiating technologies that contribute to accelerating Change, and not any one technology in particular.

Force

9

Leadership

In the first section of this book, we discussed Change, the need for Change, the Rate of Change and the importance for a company to be able to accelerate Change. And thanks to our friend Sir Isaac Newton, we are able to define acceleration using the formula **acceleration = Force ÷ mass**, or, **a = F/m**. Companies must apply enough Force to overcome its mass to accelerate Change.

In the previous section, we examined the critical components of a company's mass, namely, people, structure, processes, systems and assets. Each of these critical components have characteristics of their own *inertia* relative to their Rate of Change. Oftentimes that Rate of Change is not fast enough for a company to remain competitive. Or even worse, the *inertia* of a company's mass may even be going in the wrong direction!

In this section, we will explore the means of Force that a company can apply to overcome the *inertia* of their mass to accelerate Change. Of all the Forces at a company's disposal to accelerate Change, the most powerful of these Forces is Leadership. The most effective Leaders understand this and are proficient in their role of *accelerating Change, to achieve a result, that satisfies a need.*

Leadership is one area where a company can convert

its mass into an effective Force to accelerate Change. Leaders are people. People are a critical component of a company's mass. As previously discussed in Chapter 4, one way for a company to accelerate Change is to lower its mass by reducing the number of people it employs. In addition to lowering the denominator of the acceleration equation, another way to increase the acceleration of Change is to increase the Force, or numerator of the equation. The more effective Leaders a company has, the higher the acceleration of Change.

The impact of converting mass into Force on the acceleration equation through Leaders is shown in Figure 9.1 below:

Figure 9.1: Accelerating Change through Leaders

$$a = \frac{F}{m} \longrightarrow \text{Leaders}$$

When it comes to accelerating Change, the first job of Leadership is to make the case for Change. In other words, Leaders need to convince people <u>why</u> Change is necessary. This is not an easy job, as people often times resist Change, especially if a company is already making money and is viewed as being successful. Occasionally that resistance will escalate to fear as people perceive, rightly or wrongly, what Change may mean to them personally.

The most conducive environment for a Leader in which to make the case for Change is when a "burning platform" exists. This is when the very survival of the company is imminently at risk and that fact is broadly understood by the employees throughout the organization. After all, not only is the company at risk, but people's jobs are at risk as well. It is much easier to convince people to Change what they do and how they do it when they know that their livelihoods are at risk. This is where the fear of Change is outweighed by the pain of staying the same.

But what if a "burning platform" doesn't exit?

Clearly, making the case for Change is a much more difficult job for Leaders when no "burning platform" exists. This condition is the norm, not the exception. Over the course of my career, I have done the majority of my work with companies who are viewed as being successful. In fact, my experiences have told me that the most successful companies are those who have Leaders who are always looking for ways to accelerate Change to become even more successful.

Be that as it may, making the case for Change in successful companies is a difficult job, even for the most dynamic Leaders. These Leaders must possess and effectively utilize many attributes. They must be able to understand and manage the expectations of company ownership and, in the case of public corporations, the shareholders and "The Street." They must be able to objectively assess their company's strengths and weaknesses, vis-à-vis their competition. They must be able to translate these expectations and assessments into a well-thought-out and articulate case for Change. And they must effectively communicate the case for Change throughout their organizations to rally the troops to action, including being able to answer the employees' question, "What's in it for me?"

As part of communicating and rallying the troops, Leaders must set clear goals for their organizations regarding what Change is expected and in what timeframe. In Chapter 1, we reviewed that Change is comprised of two elements, direction and magnitude. In Chapter 2, we introduced time to establish the Rate of Change. And in Chapter 3, we showed how acceleration is an increase in the Rate of Change.

An *"Accelerator Goal,"* or simply **Accelerator,** is an extremely effective and necessary tool that should be used by all Leaders to communicate the Change that is expected to satisfy a need. The **Accelerator** must always contain the specific and measurable components of direction, magnitude and time. It should contain enough stretch so as to be viewed as a motivating call to action, yet be attainable so as not to deflate the troops by having them perceive it as being unrealistic.

Let's say that a CEO had been struggling with a stagnant North American EBITDA performance over the last several years and that the company was in danger of losing market share if the introduction of their newest product model, which had been bogged down in development, could not be introduced within the next 12 months. An example of an **Accelerator** that the CEO might craft is as follows:

> *Increase the EBITDA of our North American business by at least $100 million annually, while delivering the first 5,000 units of our newest model, by one year from now.*

This **Accelerator** contains two specific and measurable components of direction and magnitude, namely, EBITDA and units of the newest model. For EBITDA, the direction is to increase, and the magnitude is at least $100 million annually. For units of the newest model, the direction is an increase, and since the implied starting point is zero, the magnitude is 5,000 units. For both components of the **Accelerator**, the timeframe is one year, so the Rates of Change are a $100 million increase in EBITDA per year and 5,000 new model units per year.

The implication of the above example is that the Rate of Change contained in the **Accelerator** is sufficient to motivate people to take action. On the other hand, the Rate of Change should not be so large as to be perceived to be unrealistic. After all, people need to believe that the **Accelerator** is attainable in order to remain motivated to achieve it. But most importantly, the resulting Rate of Change, when achieved, must satisfy the company's need. So, although the statement of Change may sound simple, much thought and careful consideration must be used when crafting an **Accelerator.**

Accelerators are not just for CEOs! Remember, *Accelerator* is short for *"**Accelerator Goal.**"* All Leaders must be proficient in accelerating the Rate of Change within their sphere of influence, be it a team, a department, a division, or whatever formal or informal organization it may be. In fact, any person who "manages" other people is expected to be a Leader. And one of the most important attributes for any Leader is to be proficient at setting and achieving goals that accelerate the Rate of Change.

But a company cannot afford to have indiscriminate goals being pursued throughout their organizations that could potentially conflict with the **Accelerator.** In Figure 7.1, we reviewed a "Closed-Loop Managing System." It is imperative that all Leaders assure that the **Accelerator** is translated down through and across the organization, resulting in the alignment of organizational purpose, focus and achievement. The visual in Figure 9.2 demonstrates this concept.

Figure 9.2: Goal Alignment

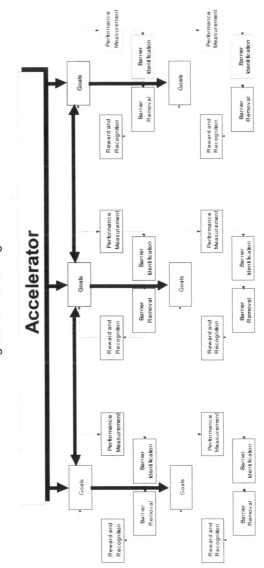

48

In addition to goal alignment, effective Leaders must have the ability to garner alignment and agreement with other Leaders in order to accelerate Change.

But who are these other Leaders? And garner Leadership agreement about what?

For now, let's just say that the "what" the Leaders have to garner agreement from other Leaders about consists of the description of the Change, in the form of the **Accelerator** or goal, plus the other components of Force that will accelerate Change (to be discussed in subsequent chapters). The other Leaders are those people in positions of influence who are affected by, or who are required to affect, the Change that is being sought. These people who have a stake in the Change, are typically and generically called "stakeholders." More specifically, these groupings of influential "stakeholders" make up "decision networks."

Decision-making is a necessary attribute of any Leader. They must be able to make decisions and take action, or no Change will occur. But making decisions and taking action unilaterally is not an effective way to win friends, influence people or affect Change. In Chapter 4, we talked about the importance of ownership as a critical link to affect Change, demonstrated in Figure 4.2. An important part of a Leader's role is to actively engage the "stakeholders" in the "decision network" to achieve their ownership and agreement to the **Accelerator** or goal, plus the other components of force to be utilized to accelerate Change.

The "stakeholders" within any "decision network" can be classified into "decision-makers," "key influencers," "vetoers" and "authorizers." The "decision-maker" is the Leader who is accountable for driving the Change, from conception, through design and all the way through implementation. It is the "decision-maker's" responsibility to gain the agreement from the other "stakeholders" in the "decision network." If this agreement is not reached, the Change being sought and the components of Force being proposed to accelerate the Change will be in jeopardy, as the non-agreeing "stakeholders" will, at minimum, not be supportive and may even actively fight against what is being proposed.

"Key influencers" are those people, most likely influential Leaders in their own right, who are either affected by the Change that is sought by the "decision-maker," or who are required to alter what they and their organizations do in order to affect the Change being sought. "Vetoers" are people who can say no, stopping the Change being sought, like a corporate attorney (sorry my legal friends!), but they cannot say yes or authorize the Change. An "authorizer" can say yes or no to the Change being sought, along with all of the components of Force being proposed to accelerate the Change.

Occasionally, the "decision-maker" and the "authorizer" can be one-in-the-same person. This can only happen if two conditions exist. First, all of the "stakeholders" in the "decision network" must reside within the organizational responsibility of the "decision-maker." And second, the "decision-maker" must be at a level within the organization that is high enough to authorize the Change and all of the components of Force being proposed to accelerate the Change. These conditions rarely exist.

Because these conditions rarely exist, it is incumbent upon the "decision-maker" to identify all of the "stakeholders" in the "decision network" and classify them according to their roles as "key influencers," "vetoers," or "authorizers." Once identified, it is crucial for the "decision-maker" to achieve Leadership alignment by gaining the agreement of the other "stakeholders" in the "decision network" to the **Accelerator** or goal, plus all of the components of Force for accelerating Change beyond Leadership.

These other components of Force include a Vision, Discovery, a Roadmap, a Business Case, Execution and Cash.

10

Vision

In the previous Chapter, we introduced the *Accelerator Goal,"* or **Accelerator**, as the definition of the Change needed in terms of direction, magnitude and timing. The **Accelerator** is fashioned in the form of measures or metrics. It is a result, when achieved. Remember, the primary role of Leadership is *accelerating Change, to achieve a result, that satisfies a need.* But the **Accelerator** is not a descriptor of the attributes of the Change needed.

In order for "stakeholders" and others to relate to the case for Change, they need to be able to see what's different in the way business is to be conducted in the future in order to achieve the **Accelerator.** They need to be able to envision what the destination is, otherwise, "any road will get them there." A well-designed and agreed to Vision of a company's future state is a powerful Force for accelerating Change.

So what's a well-designed Vision? And how do you get it agreed to?

A well-designed Vision should be just that, visual. It should utilize the old saying, "A picture is worth a thousand words." Most people can relate to pictures if they're easy to understand and are put together in a way that tells an effective story, when also supported by the right words. Additionally, it helps if the Vision can be arranged on one sheet of paper, albeit a large sheet of paper. Effective large-scale visual graphics also facilitate the process of gaining agreement from the "stakeholders." But more on that later.

The Vision should have a title that embodies the theme of the Vision's intent. The title should be insightful and meaningful to all "stakeholders." It must be thoughtfully crafted, so as to avoid being viewed through the cynical eyes of potential critics.

The Vision must show what's different from today in terms of the components of company mass that are pertinent to the need being addressed in the Vision, namely, people, structure, processes, systems and/or assets. This difference can be implied, by only showing the future state. Or the difference can be explicit, by incorporating a "from-to" format.

The pictures and words contained in the Vision should describe, at a high level, the attributes of the critical components of the company's mass in the future state. So whether it's a simplified organization structure with higher spans-of-control, or "pull" versus "push" manufacturing processes, or "Closed-Loop Managing Systems," or a consolidated footprint of the warehouses in a distribution network, etc., the Vision must describe the future state of a company's mass in enough detail so people can see and understand the Changes needed. There should be no ambiguity.

Most importantly, the Vision must be designed so that, when implemented, it achieves the **Accelerator**!

The design of the Vision is the accountability of the Leader who is the "decision-maker" in the "decision network." The "decision-maker" does not have to go-it-alone. He or she can delegate the actual work of preparing the

53

Vision "map" to others in their organization or to outside consultants, but the "decision-maker" must <u>own</u> the Vision and be passionate about it.

But the best designed Vision in the world is of no use if the other "stakeholders" in the "decision network" do not agree with it. The "decision-maker" must also be accountable for achieving alignment with the other "stakeholders" by gaining their agreement to the Vision. In my experience, the best and quickest way to secure agreement to a Vision is through the employment of a technique called "rapid prototype—multiple iteration," using large-scale visual graphics, called "maps."

The "rapid prototype—multiple iteration" technique can be viewed in Figure 10.1 below:

Figure 10.1: Rapid Prototype – Multiple Iteration

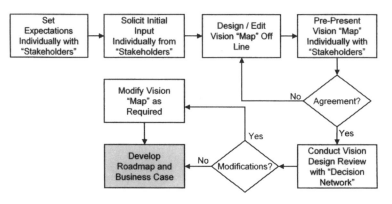

The "decision-maker" needs to set the expectations for the other "stakeholders" in the "decision network" around what will be required of them in their journey to develop the Vision. This includes their expected roles and levels of participation. It is best to do this individually with "stakeholders" so you can tailor the message to the personal needs of each person. Plus they will feel more free to voice their potential issues and concerns privately, which you will want to know about early on so you can deal with them effectively and avoid potential conflicts later on.

The next step is to individually solicit the initial input from all "stakeholders" regarding their view of the future. This can be done interview-style, through well-thought-out and designed Visioning questions. Once the inputs from the interviews are gathered, a first draft of the Vision "map" can be quickly constructed (rapid prototype) by the "decision-maker's" staff or consultants, naturally under his or her direction.

The next step is perhaps the most important step and is oftentimes overlooked. It is imperative to conduct individual pre-present meetings with the "stakeholders" to review the first draft of the Vision "map." The intent is to incorporate their ideas (ownership) and to surface and address their issues and concerns with the Vision privately. The last thing that you want, as a Leader and "decision-maker," is to have a "key influencer," a "vetoer," or, worse yet, an "authorizer," disagree with your Vision in a public forum. It is much more difficult and time-consuming to recover after public criticism and, conversely, it is much easier to achieve Leadership alignment after individually attending to the needs of each "stakeholder" in the "decision network" until they agree with the Vision (multiple iteration).

Once the pre-presents are concluded and the "stakeholders" individually have their fingerprints on the design of the Vision "map," the "decision-maker" should conduct a design review meeting with the entire "decision network." Since all have agreed individually to the Vision, the Vision "map" should require only minor modifications, if any, at this point. Plus the design review meeting builds *energy* and *momentum* (two more of Newton's terms) when "stakeholders" see their peers agreeing to the Vision in a public forum. The "decision-maker" has now achieved agreement to the Vision and can proceed directly with the two subsequent components of Force to accelerate Change, an implementation Roadmap and a Business Case.

But before we go there, we need to visit a component of Force that should be applied simultaneously with the Vision, that being Discovery.

11

Discovery

Assessing the "current state" of a company's mass, namely, people, structure, processes, systems and assets, formulates the baseline for a Leader's case for Change and establishes the "starting point" for the Change journey. The primary purpose of this assessment is to identify, or Discover, what the barriers are to implementing the Vision and achieving the **Accelerator.** A comprehensive and accurate "starting point" Discovery is a necessary Force for accelerating Change.

But what is "starting point" Discovery?

"Starting point" Discovery is the application of diagnostic tools designed to comprehensively and accurately profile the "current state" of a company's mass. These diagnostic tools can include surveys, interviews, process mapping, functional checklists, work sampling, day-in-the-life studies, span-of-control studies, overall equipment effectiveness (OEE) studies, etc. These diagnostic tools need to be professionally designed and applied, assuring they are tailored to the specific needs of the Leader and focused on the Change that is being sought in the **Accelerator.**

"Starting point" Discovery also involves the analysis of both operating and financial data, as it pertains to the **Accelerator.** Trends and variations in performance are studied in order to establish baselines for improvement. This will be discussed more in Chapter 13 dealing with Business Case.

Although data analysis is critical, and my benchmarking friends are not going to like this one, I am not a proponent of extensive benchmarking studies as a means for accelerating Change. They are typically too long in duration and their results are inconclusive due to the fact that no two companies are alike. However, I am a proponent of Leaders using readily accessible information about their competition that exists in the public domain in order to help them make the case for Change and establish an **Accelerator.**

Based on the findings and conclusions from the diagnostics and data analyses, the barriers to implementing the Vision and achieving the **Accelerator** should be easily identified and documented. It is the responsibility of the "decision-maker" to achieve Leadership alignment by getting the other "stakeholders" in the "decision network" to agree to the list of barriers. This can be accomplished through individual pre-presents of the findings and conclusions, followed by a group Discovery meeting.

Taking a closer look at a barrier, it is really an attribute of the mass of a company's "current state." Just one example of what oftentimes are dozens of barriers could be, "there are no 'Closed-Loop Managing Systems' at the lowest levels of the organization." Typically, the inverse of a barrier is an attribute that you would want to see contained in the "future state" Vision, in this case, "Closed-Loop Managing Systems" at the front-line supervisory level of the organization. For this reason, although "starting point" Discovery can be launched simultaneously with the "rapid prototype—multiple iteration" approach to create the Vision, it should conclude prior to the final version of the Vision. In this way, the inverse of the barriers can be incorporated into the Vision "map" as attributes of the future state.

Leaders must properly position the intent of "starting point" Discovery within their organizations at the outset. Although it is necessary to take an honest and critical "look in the mirror," "starting point" Discovery should not be used as a backward-looking exercise to find fault, place blame, or indict anyone. Its purpose is to take a snapshot of the "current state" in order to identify the barriers that must be overcome in order to realize the Vision and **Accelerator**. Discovery very much has forward-looking intentions. Understanding these intentions is paramount to motivate people to openly and honestly participate in "starting point" Discovery, making it a positive Force for accelerating Change.

12

Roadmap

Once the "starting point" (point A) has been determined through Discovery and the Vision of the "future state" has been set (point B), a well-designed and <u>agreed upon</u> Roadmap is the next component of Force for accelerating the Change and achieving the **Accelerator.** Similar to the Vision, the implementation Roadmap must be agreed to by all of the "stakeholders" in the "decision network," and the Leader responsible for doing this is still the "decision-maker." The "rapid prototype—multiple iteration" technique shown in Figure 10.1, and enabled by a large-scale visual graphic, or "map," should also be utilized to achieve the agreement to the Roadmap. Without this agreement, Change will not happen!

The Roadmap should directly reflect the approach to be utilized to implement the components of the Vision and the achievement of the **Accelerator.** The components, of which there are typically many, can be combined into logical groupings. These groupings will then drive individual initiatives, also called streams of work, or more simply, "workstreams." If the linkage between the Vision and the Roadmap approach can not be clearly seen, then the Roadmap will not be an effective Force for accelerating Change, as it will not be seen as credible.

The list shown in Figure 12.1 on page 61 contains the

fundamental elements of the implementation Roadmap that must be agreed to by all of the "stakeholders" in the "decision network":

Figure 12.1: Roadmap Elements

- Workstreams and Activities
- Sequencing ad Timing
- Key Milestones and Deliverables
- Implementation Organization and Governance
- Implementation Resources (internal and external)
- Team Members' Roles and Responsibilities
- Communication Plan
- Initiatives Integration
- Business Case Tracking

Most people are already familiar with the fundamental elements listed above to some extent. So, although they are all quite important, I will not expound upon them here, with one exception. That exception is initiatives integration, which is oftentimes overlooked as a critical success factor to accelerating Change.

Most large companies and corporations have multiple initiatives in play at any given point in time. Sometimes these initiatives can number into the hundreds, and a healthy dose of initiatives rationalization is in order. But that is a whole other topic, and not directly part of this discussion. However, it is highly likely that there will be a number of legitimate initiatives already underway that will either impact the Roadmap to be implemented, or, conversely, be impacted by it.

When identifying the initiatives requiring integration, there are many types to look for. They can be targeted on any component of a company's mass. So existing initiatives could include things like: hiring campaigns or training programs (people), post-acquisition integration or restructuring efforts (structure), new product introductions or process redesigns (processes), information systems installations or modifications (systems), new equipment installations or plant closures (assets), etc. These are the types of initiatives that must be identified, preferably during the "starting point" Discovery period, and "integrated" (more on the "integration" topic in Chapter 14: Execution) with the "workstreams" contained in the implementation Roadmap.

When designing the Roadmap, it is advantageous, if possible, to build in some opportunities for "early successes." If some meaningful accomplishments can occur quickly, they can be recognized and trumpeted to the rest of the organization. If done well and not superficial, this can motivate the entire organization and increase the *energy* and *momentum* toward **accelerating Change, to achieve a result, that satisfies a need.**

13

Business Case

A compelling Business Case, that justifies embarking upon the Roadmap to implement the Vision and achieve the **Accelerator** is another Force for accelerating Change. The implementation of the Vision can oftentimes require significant investment of the company's resources, in terms of both people and money. The "authorizer" in the "decision network" is the person who resides at a high enough level within the organization to approve the required level of investment. Depending on the magnitude of the investments required, this could involve securing the approval of the company's Board of Directors.

The Leader who is the "decision-maker" in the "decision network" is the person who is accountable for securing the approval for the required investments. Since there is typically intense competition for the company's resources by many of its Leaders, the "decision-maker" will typically require the agreement of all of the "stakeholders" in the "decision network" to the proposed Business Case. Like with the Vision and the Roadmap, the "rapid prototype—multiple iteration" technique, using a Business Case "map," is the most effective means of garnering this agreement, in my experience.

The Business Case must delineate the areas where benefits are expected to be achieved. These areas of benefits could come in the form of recurring benefits that impact the company's P&L statement year-on-year, like direct labor, materials, energy, etc. The areas of benefits could also come in the form of one-time benefits that impact the company's balance sheet, like inventories and receivables. These areas of benefits must be uniquely and logically linked to the specific Vision that is being implemented.

Once the areas of benefits have been identified, based on implementing the Vision, the magnitude and timing of the benefits need to be projected, given the timeframes laid out in the implementation Roadmap. If the benefits are of the recurring nature, then they need to be offset by any additional recurring costs. The projections of benefits, both recurring and one-time, then need to be offset by the required one-time investments necessary to implement the Vision, in order to develop a profile of the cumulative net Cash flow.

The graph shown in Figure 13.1 below shows an example of a cumulative net Cash flow of a compelling Business Case:

Figure 13.1: Cumulative Net Cash Flow

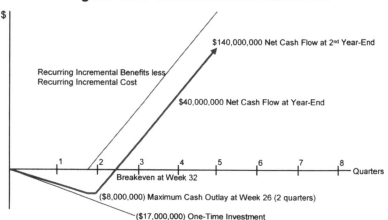

64

In the above example, the annual recurring P&L benefits are $100,000,000, with a one-time implementation investment of $17,000,000, yielding a 5.9:1 return on investment. The break-even point occurs 32 weeks following the launch of the Roadmap, and the maximum Cash outlay of ($8,000,000) occurs 26 weeks, or two quarters, following the Roadmap's launching.

Many Leaders within companies and corporations are under tremendous pressure from their bosses, including the Board of Directors, and "The Street" to make their quarterly profit or budget projections, more commonly known as their quarterly numbers. Unfortunately, these pressures can oftentimes freeze would-be Leaders into inaction, in fear of not meeting their quarterly numbers in the short term, and sacrificing the long-term good of the company in the process. This risk exists in the example shown in Figure 13.1 on the previous page. Welcome to the pressures of Leadership!

I have occasionally done work for some very well-run mutual insurance companies and privately held companies that don't suffer from these same pressures. Their Leaders are freer to take the longer-term view and not be as concerned with making their short-term quarterly numbers. But these companies are exceptions, not the rule.

Getting Leaders to take action, even in the face of short-term quarterly numbers misses, is why an extremely compelling Business Case is nearly always a necessary component of Force to accelerate Change.

14

Execution

A wise corporate Chairman and CEO who I was doing work for once told me, "Execution is my strategy." For those of you who hadn't noticed, this is the first time I have used the word "strategy" in this book. Sorry, my strategy friends! But the Chairman and CEO's point to me was clear, that being, the best strategy in the world is worthless if the company is not capable of making it happen.

Now don't get me wrong, it is of critical importance for a company to decide on what businesses they should be in, what markets they should enter or exit, what customer segments they should target, what products and services they should offer, and what channels they should sell through. But deciding on these strategic issues doesn't automatically, like magic, make them happen. This is why, like my client told me long ago, Execution is a powerful Force for accelerating Change.

Some companies have had long-standing strategies that don't materially deviate. Other companies seem to be constantly shifting their strategy. Any shift in strategy will undoubtedly require corresponding Changes in the capabilities and capacities of the company's mass, namely, people, structure, processes, systems and assets, in order to pull it off. So while strategy can help a Leader make the case for Change, I have found that the strategy needs to subsequently be translated into an **Accelerator,** a Vision, Discovery, a Roadmap and a Business Case, in order to effectively accelerate the Change required for Execution, otherwise the strategy is useless.

The Force of Execution deals largely with implementing the Roadmap in a way that efficiently and effectively realizes the Vision and **Accelerator.**

In Chapter 12, we reviewed how Roadmaps are comprised of "workstreams" designed to implement the Vision and achieve the **Accelerator.** It is important that each "workstream" be staffed by a Leader and supported by a team of appropriate internal and external resources. The team resources should possess the skills and experience to deal with the "workstream's" subject matter and approach. More importantly, these resources should be positive, credible and well-respected people, who are persuasive communicators, creative, and are open-minded problem solvers and good team players. In short, they should be Leaders also.

There must be a governing body that provides guidance and coaching to the "workstream" teams. The governing body should review, and either approve or revise, the recommendations advanced to them by the "workstream" teams. More often than not, the governing body should be comprised by many, if not all, of the "stakeholders" in the "decision network." Governing body members must be able to commit to meet on a regular basis, usually at least monthly, to fulfill their duties.

In order to engage "workstream" team members and keep them motivated, they should have a high sense of ownership over what they do and how they do it. The first way to do this is allow them to build their own team charters, within a prescribed format to include, goals, scope, membership, approach, timelines, deliverables, etc. Another way to gain team members' ownership is to have them develop their own large-scale Vision "maps," Roadmaps and Business Case "maps" for each of their respective "workstreams." Naturally, the team charters and "maps" must be sanctioned by the governing body.

Also in Chapter 12, we introduced the subject of initiatives integration. Initiatives integration starts by cataloguing those initiatives that intersect the Roadmap to be implemented. Integrating with other initiatives involves forming relationships with influential "stakeholders" involved in those initiatives and working with them to identify the critical interface points. By critical interface points, I'm referring to the specific inputs and outputs, also called dependencies, across the initiatives that are required to effectively execute the respective initiatives within the expected timeframes. The active managing of these dependencies, depending on the number of initiatives involved, can require a "workstream" in and of itself, supported by an initiatives integration "map."

There has been much written about effective project management, so I will not indulge you in that topic. However, focused, dedicated and proficient project Leadership is critical to effective Execution. Project Leadership must be proficient in two directions. First, in order to effectively Lead the "workstream" teams, the project Leader must have excellent interpersonal skills, yet be task-oriented, focused on the timely Execution of the Roadmap deliverables. Second, the project Leader must continually strive to achieve the alignment of the "stakeholders" in the "decision network" to all "workstream" deliverables being implemented. The role of project Leader requires unique skills and capabilities, and, oftentimes, is best filled by a professional who does this for a living.

Another critical aspect of Execution is communications. Again, this is a subject matter that has been much written about. Like initiatives integration, communications oftentimes deserves its own "workstream," supported by its own communications "map." The communications "map" should identify all of the key constituencies that needed to be communicated to, along with the timing, source and media for all key messages to be delivered. Remember, the purpose of the key messages is to motivate each constituency to support Execution!

The final component of Execution that needs to be highlighted is performance tracking and management. The concept of goal alignment was displayed in Figure 9.2. In fact, what is really displayed there is a series of integrated "Closed-Loop Managing Systems." In Chapter 7, we talked about how effective managing systems, as opposed to information systems alone, can be a powerful Force for accelerating Change.

The ultimate measure of successful Execution is the achievement of the **Accelerator.**

It is imperative that the required series of integrated "Closed-Loop Managing Systems" be implemented to track the daily and weekly performance versus the goals, and drive corrective action when required. This performance attainment tracking should be tied into the monthly financials, both the P&L statement and, when Changes in assets is being sought, the balance sheet. Leaders who can drive the implementation of "Closed-Loop Managing Systems" provide a sustaining capability to their respective companies to Execute Change against future **Accelerators.**

15

Cash

Way back when, at Purdue University, the Department Head of the School of Industrial Engineering, who was the professor of one of my classes, walked into the classroom the first day of the semester. He didn't say "good morning, class," as most professors did back then. He didn't even look at the class. Instead, he turned his back to us and went to the blackboard, where he drew a large symbol. The symbol he chose to draw as his opening message to the class was as follows:

Then he turned around and exclaimed, "This is what it's all about!"

He told us that <u>the</u> reason that companies were in business was to make money. He went on to say that the only reason why a company would hire any of us was to help them to make more money. He provided us with a very clear message and a very visual picture.

A company's ability to make money is its primary purpose and a measure of its success. No matter what other stated purposes that a company has, be they providing employment in the community, protecting the environment, or even for philanthropic reasons, none of these purposes can be served without first serving the fundamental purpose of a company, that being to make money. And the Cash that a company makes can absolutely be utilized as a significant Force to accelerate Change.

Not only can Cash be used to pay down a company's current liabilities and long-term debt, it can also be used to bolster a company's competitiveness in their areas of need. Depending on the company's need, Cash can be used to invest in new technologies, or engineers, or new products and services, or to break into new markets, or to launch new productivity improvement programs, or to acquire competitors, or to . . . well, you get the picture. When used the right way, Cash is a powerful Force to accelerate Change.

This brings us right back to Leadership. It is up to a company's Leaders to determine and apply the best use of the company's Cash. In fact, Leadership drives all of the other components of Force, be it Vision, Discovery, Roadmap, Business Case, Execution, or even Cash. Leadership is the most powerful Force a company can possess to accelerate Change.

And the most important role for a company's Leaders, be they a CEO, a first-line supervisor, or anyone in between, is to focus their Leadership on *accelerating Change, to achieve a result, that satisfies a need!*

Epilogue

I really need to go back to Westminster Abbey and revisit Sir Isaac Newton's grave. First of all, I owe him an apology for the rude way I "talked" to him on my previous visit. Secondly, I need to thank him for providing me with a framework, namely, **Force = mass x acceleration**, to organize my thoughts about accelerating Change within companies and corporations.

But most importantly, I want to promise him that I will passionately pursue the advancement of this approach to help Leaders perform their most important role of **accelerating Change, to achieve a result, that satisfies a need!**

The following is my "future state" Vision for advancing Corporate Physics to Leaders:

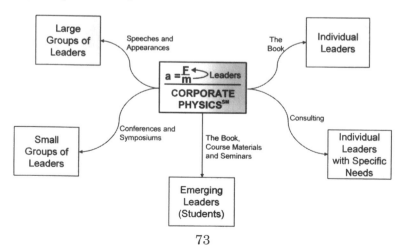

About the Author

John Calvello has over thirty-five years of business experience, ***accelerating Change, to achieve a result, that satisfies a need***. He has personally analyzed, designed, sold, and implemented needs-based Change programs for hundreds of companies across multiple industries. These programs have integrated initiatives involving people, structure, processes, systems, and assets required for successful Change.

Mr. Calvello was the driving force in developing an innovative methodology called High Velocity Management (HVM), a predecessor to Lean Enterprise. For over a decade, he has also conceived and honed a unique approach that has helped top executives create the "case for change" by gaining broad agreement to a future state vision, an implementation roadmap and a business case, all using large-scale visual mapping. The consulting projects launched out of the application of this unique approach have benefitted his clients' companies by billions of dollars over the years.

The author is now introducing *Corporate Physics* as the most innovative approach to date for ***accelerating Change, to achieve a result, that satisfies a need.***

Mr. Calvello earned his Bachelor of Science degree in Industrial Engineering from Purdue University in 1973. He lives in Naples, Florida with his wife, Mary Anne.

For more information, please visit www.corporatephysics.com.